Christs Victorie & Triumph in Heaven and Earth, Over & After Death by Giles Fletcher

Giles Fletcher was born around 1586.

He was also known as Giles Fletcher the Younger as his father went by the same name. The family was certainly an illustrious one in literary circles. He was the brother of Phineas Fletcher and the cousin of John Fletcher. His father, Giles Fletcher the Elder, is best remembered for the Elizabethan sonnet cycle Licia.

Educated at Westminster school and then to Trinity College, Cambridge. He remained in Cambridge after his ordination and became a Reader in Greek Grammar in 1615 and then a Reader in Greek Language in 1618. In 1619 left to become rector of Alderton in Suffolk.

His most well-known work is Christ's Victorie and Triumph, in Heaven, in Earth, over and after Death, and comprises of four cantos. The first, Christ's Victory in Heaven, concerns a dispute in heaven between justice and mercy, using the facts of Christ's life on earth; the second, Christ's Victory on Earth, deals with an allegorical account of Christ's Temptation; the third, Christ's Triumph over Death, covers the Passion; and the fourth, Christ's Triumph after Death, covers the Resurrection and Ascension and ends with an affectionate eulogy of his brother Phineas as Thyrsilis.

The work is written in the style of Edmund Spenser and Milton was generous in his use of the work in his own Paradise Regained.

Index of Contents

CANTO I

The birth of him that no beginning knewe,
Yet gives beginning to all that are borne,
And how the Infinite farre greater grewe,
By growing lesse, and how the rising Morne,
That shot from heav'n, did backe to heaven retourne,
The obsequies of him that could not die,
And death of life, ende of eternitie,
How worthily he died, that died unworthily;

How God, and Man did both embrace each other,
Met in one person, heav'n, and earth did kiss,
And how a Virgin did become a Mother,

And bare that Sonne, who the worlds Father is,
And Maker of his mother, and how Bliss
Descended from the bosome of the High,
To cloath himselfe in naked miserie,
Sayling at length to heav'n, in earth, triumphantly,

Is the first flame, wherewith my whiter Muse
Doth burne in heavenly love, such love to tell.
O thou that didst this holy fire infuse,
And taught'st this brest, but late the grave of hell,
Wherein a blind, and dead heart liv'd, to swell
With better thoughts, send downe those lights that lend
Knowledge, how to begin, and how to end
The love, that never was, nor ever can be pend.

Ye sacred writings in whose antique leaves
The memories of heav'n entreasur'd lie,
Say, what might be the cause that Mercie heaves
The dust of sinne above th' industrious skie;
And lets it not to dust, and ashes flie?
Could Justice be of sinne so over-wooed,
Or so great ill be cause of so great good,
That bloody man to save, mans Saviour shed his blood?

Or did the lips of Mercie droppe soft speech
For traytrous man, when at th' Eternalls throne
Incensed Nemesis did heav'n beseech
With thundring voice, that justice might be showne
Against the Rebells, that from God were flowne;
O say, say how could Mercie plead for those
That scarcely made, against their Maker rose?
Will any slay his friend, that he may spare his foes?

There is a place beyond that flaming hill
From whence the starres their thin apparance shed,
A place, beyond all place, where never ill,
Nor impure thought was ever harboured,
But Sainctly Heroes are for ever s'ed
To keepe an everlasting Sabbaoths rest,
Still wishing that, of what th' ar still possest,
Enjoying but one joy, but one of all joyes best.

Here, when the ruine of that beauteous frame,
Whose golden building shin'd with everie starre
Of excellence, deform'd with age became,
Mercy, remembring peace in midst of warre,
Lift up the musique of her voice, to barre
Eternall fate, least it should quite erace

That from the world, which was the first worlds grace,
And all againe into their nothing, Chaos chase.

For what had all this All, which Man in one
Did not unite; the earth, aire, water, fire,
Life, sense, and spirit, nay the powrefull throne
Of the divinest Essence, did retire,
And his owne Image into clay inspire:
So that this Creature well might called be
Of the great world, the small epitomie,
Of the dead world, the live, and quicke anatomie.

But Justice had no sooner Mercy seene
Smoothing the wrinkles of her Fathers browe,
But up she starts, and throwes her selfe betweene.
As when a vapour, from a moory slough,
Meeting with fresh Eous, that but now
Open'd the world, which all in darkenesse lay,
Doth heav'ns bright face of his rayes disaray,
And sads the smiling orient of the springing day.

She was a Virgin of austere regard,
Not as the world esteemes her, deafe, and blind,
But as the Eagle, that hath oft compar'd
Her eye with heav'ns, so, and more brightly shin'd
Her lamping sight: for she the same could winde
Into the solid heart, and with her eares,
The silence of the thought loude speaking heares,
And in one hand a paire of even scoals she weares.

No riot of affection revell kept
Within her brest, but a still apathy
Possessed all her soule, which softly slept,
Securely, without tempest, no sad crie
Awakes her pittie, but wrong'd povertie,
Sending his eyes to heav'n swimming in teares,
With hideous clamours ever struck her eares,
Whetting the blazing sword, that in her hand she beares.

The winged Lightning is her Mercury,
And round about her mightie thunders sound:
Impatient of himselfe lies pining by
Pale Sicknes, with his kercher'd head upwound,
And thousand noysome plagues attend her round,
But if her clowdie browe but once growe foule,
The flints doe melt, and rocks to water rowle,
And ayrie mountaines shake, and frighted shadowes howle.

Famine, and bloodles Care, and bloodie Warre,
Want, and the Want of knowledge how to use
Abundance, Age, and Feare, that runnes afarre
Before his fellowe Greefe, that aye pursues
His winged steps; for who would not refuse
Greefes companie, a dull, and rawebon'd spright,
That lankes the cheekes, and pales the freshest sight,
Unbosoming the cheerefull brest of all delight;

Before this cursed throng, goes Ignorance,
That needes will leade the way he cannot see:
And after all, Death doeth his flag advaunce,
And in the mid'st, Strife still would roaguing be,
Whose ragged flesh, and cloaths did well agree:
And round about, amazed Horror flies,
And over all, Shame veiles his guiltie eyes,
And underneth, Hells hungrie throat still yawning lies.

Upon two stonie tables, spread before her,
She lean'd her bosome, more then stonie hard,
There slept th' unpartiall judge, and strict restorer
Of wrong, or right, with paine, or with reward,
There hung the skore of all our debts, the card
Whear good, and bad, and life, and death were painted:
Was never heart of mortall so untainted,
But when that scroule was read, with thousand terrors fainted.

Witnes the thunder that mount Sinai heard,
When all the hill with firie clouds did flame,
And wandring Israel, with the sight afeard,
Blinded with seeing, durst not touch the same,
But like a wood of shaking leaves became.
On this dead Justice, she, the Living Lawe,
Bowing herselfe with a majestique awe,
All heav'n, to heare her speech, did into silence drawe.

Dread Lord of Spirits, well thou did'st devise
To fling the worlds rude dunghill, and the drosse
Of the ould Chaos, farthest from the skies,
And thine owne seate, that heare the child of losse,
Of all the lower heav'n the curse, and crosse,
That wretch, beast, caytive, monster Man, might spend,
(Proude of the mire, in which his soule is pend)
Clodded in lumps of clay, his wearie life to end.

His bodie dust: whear grewe such cause of pride?
His soule thy Image: what could he enuie?
Himselfe most happie: if he so would bide:

Now grow'n most wretched, who can remedie?
He slewe himselfe, himselfe the enemie.
That his owne soule would her owne murder wreake,
If I were silent, heav'n and earth would speake,
And if all fayl'd, these stones would into clamours breake.

How many darts made furrowes in his side,
When she, that out of his owne side was made,
Gave feathers to their flight? whear was the pride
Of their newe knowledge; whither did it fade,
When, running from thy voice into the shade,
He fled thy sight, himselfe of sight bereav'd;
And for his shield a leavie armour weav'd,
With which, vain ma, he thought Gods eies to have deceav'd?

And well he might delude those eyes, that see,
And judge by colours: for who ever sawe
A man of leaves, a reasonable tree?
But those that from this stocke their life did drawe,
Soone made their Father godly, and by lawe
Proclaimed Trees almightie: Gods of wood,
Of stocks, and stones with crownes of laurell stood
Templed, and fed by fathers with their childrens blood.

The sparkling fanes, that burne in beaten gould,
And, like the starres of heav'n in mid'st of night,
Blacke Egypt, as her mirrhours, doth behould,
Are but the denns whear idoll-snakes delight
Againe to cover Satan from their sight:
Yet these are all their gods, to whome they vie
The Crocodile, the Cock, the Rat, the Flie.
Fit gods, indeede, for such men to be served by.

The Fire, the winde, the sea, the sunne, and moone,
The flitting Aire, and the swift-winged How'rs,
And all the watchmen, that so nimbly runne,
And centinel about the walled towers
Of the worlds citie, in their heav'nly bowr's.
And, least their pleasant gods should want delight,
Neptune spues out the Lady Aphrodite,
And but in heaven proude Junos peacocks skorne to lite.

The senselesse Earth, the Serpent, dog, and catte,
And woorse then all these, Man, and woorst of men
Usurping Jove, and swilling Bacchus fat,
And drunke with the vines purple blood, and then
The Fiend himselfe they conjure from his denne,
Because he onely yet remain'd to be

Woorse then the worst of men, they flie from thee,
And weare his altar-stones out with their pliant knee.

All that he speakes (and all he speakes are lies)
Are oracles, 'tis he (that wounded all)
Cures all their wounds, he (that put out their eyes)
That gives them light, he (that death first did call
Into the world) that with his orizall,
Inspirits earth: he heav'ns al-seeing eye,
He earths great Prophet, he, whom rest doth flie,
That on salt billowes doth, as pillowes, sleeping lie.

But let him in his cabin restles rest,
The dungeon of darke flames, and freezing fire,
Justice in heav'n against man makes request
To God, and of his Angels doth require
Sinnes punishment: if what I did desire,
Or who, or against whome, or why, or whear,
Of, or before whom ignorant I wear,
Then should my speech their sands of sins to mountaines rear.

Wear not the heav'ns pure, in whose courts I sue,
The Judge, to whom I sue, just to requite him,
The cause for sinne, the punishment most due,
Justice her selfe the plaintiffe to endite him,
The Angells holy, before whom I cite him,
He against whom, wicked, unjust, impure;
Then might he sinnefull live, and die secure,
Or triall might escape, or triall might endure,

The Judge might partiall be, and over-pray'd,
The place appeald from, in whose courts he sues,
The fault excus'd, or punishment delayd,
The parties selfe accus'd, that did accuse,
Angels for pardon might their praiers use:
But now no starre can shine, no hope be got.
Most wretched creature, if he knewe his lot,
And yet more wretched farre, because he knowes it not.

What should I tell how barren earth is growne,
All for to sterve her children, didst not thou
Water with heav'nly showers her wombe unsowne,
And drop downe cloudes of flow'rs, didst not thou bowe
Thine easie eare unto the plowmans vowe,
Long might he looke, and looke, and long in vaine
Might load his harvest in an emptie wayne,
And beat the woods, to finde the poore okes hungrie graine.

The swelling sea seethes in his angrie waves,
And smites the earth, that dares the traytors nourish,
Yet oft his thunder their light corke outbraves,
Mowing the mountaines, on whose temples flourish
Whole woods of garlands, and, their pride to cherish,
Plowe through the seaes greene fields, and nets display
To catch the flying winds, and steale away,
Coozning the greedie sea, prisning their nimble prey.

How often have I seene the waving pine,
Tost on a watrie mountaine, knocke his head
At heav'ns too patient gates, and with salt brine
Quench the Moones burning hornes, and safely fled
From heav'ns revenge, her passengers, all dead
With stiffe astonishment, tumble to hell?
How oft the sea all earth would overswell,
Did not thy sandie girdle binde the mightie well?

Would not the aire be fill'd with steames of death,
To poyson the quicke rivers of their blood,
Did not thy windes fan, with their panting breath,
The flitting region? would not the hastie flood
Emptie it selfe into the seas wide wood,
Did'st not thou leade it wandring from his way,
To give men drinke, and make his waters strey,
To fresh the flowrie medowes, through whose fields they play?

Who makes the sources of the silver fountaines
From the flints mouth, and rocky valleis slide,
Thickning the ayrie bowells of the mountaines?
Who hath the wilde heards of the forrest tide
In their cold denns, making them hungrie bide
Till man to rest be laid? can beastly he,
That should have most sense, onely senseles be,
And all things else, beside himselfe, so awefull see?

Wear he not wilder then the salvage beast,
Prowder then haughty hills, harder then rocks,
Colder then fountaines, from their springs releast,
Lighter then aire, blinder then senseles stocks,
More changing then the rivers curling locks,
If reason would not, sense would soone reproove him,
And unto shame, if not to sorrow, moove him,
To see cold floods, wild beasts, dul stocks, hard stones out-love him.

Under the weight of sinne the earth did fall,
And swallowed Dathan; and the raging winde,
And stormie sea, and gaping Whale, did call

For Jonas; and the aire did bullets finde,
And shot from heav'n a stony showre, to grinde
The five proud Kings, that for their idols fought,
The Sunne it selfe stood still to fight it out,
And fire fro heav'n flew downe, when sin to heav'n did shout.

Should any to himselfe for safety flie?
The way to save himselfe, if any were,
Wear to flie from himselfe: should he relie
Upon the promise of his wife? but there,
What can he see, but that he most may feare,
A Syren, sweete to death: upon his friends?
Who that he needs, or that he hath not lends?
Or wanting aide himselfe, ayde to another sends?

His strength? but dust: his pleasure? cause of paine:
His hope? false courtier: youth, or beawtie? brittle:
Intreatie? fond: repentance? late, and vaine:
Just recompence? the world wear all too little:
Thy love? he hath no title to a tittle:
Hells force? in vaine her furies hell shall gather: ·
His Servants, Kinsmen, or his children rather?
His child, if good, shall judge, if bad, shall curse his father.

His life? that brings him to his end, and leaves him:
His ende? that leaves him to beginne his woe:
His goods? what good in that, that so deceaves him?
His gods of wood? their feete, alas, are slowe
To goe to helpe, that must be help't to goe:
Honour, great woorth? ah, little woorth they be
Unto their owners: wit? that makes him see
He wanted wit, that thought he had it, wanting thee.

The sea to drinke him quicke? that casts hi[m] dead:
Angells to spare? they punish: night to hide?
The world shall burne in light: the heav'ns to spread
Their wings to save him? heav'n it selfe shall slide,
And rowle away like melting starres, that glide
Along their oylie threads: his minde pursues him:
His house to shrowde, or hills to fall, and bruse him?
As Seargeants both attache, and witnesses accuse him:

What need I urge, what they must needs confesse?
Sentence on them, condemn'd by their owne lust;
I crave no more, and thou canst give no lesse,
Then death to dead men, justice to unjust;
Shame to most shamefull, and most shameles dust:
But if thy Mercie needs will spare her friends,

Let Mercie there begin, where Justice endes.
Tis cruell Mercie, that the wrong from right defends.

She ended, and the heav'nly Hierarchies,
Burning in zeale, thickly imbranded weare:
Like to an armie, that allarum cries,
And every one shakes his ydraded speare,
And the Almighties selfe, as he would teare
The earth, and her firme basis quite in sunder,
Flam'd all in just revenge, and mightie thunder,
Heav'n stole it selfe from earth by clouds that moisterd under.

As when the cheerfull Sunne, elamping wide,
Glads all the world with his uprising raye,
And wooes the widow'd earth afresh to pride,
And paint[s] her bosome with the flowrie Maye,
His silent sister steales him quite away,
Wrap't in a sable clowde, from mortall eyes,
The hastie starres at noone begin to rise,
And headlong to his early roost the sparrowe flies.

But soone as he againe dishadowed is,
Restoring the blind world his blemish't sight,
As though another day wear newely ris,
The cooz'ned birds busily take their flight,
And wonder at the shortnesse of the night:
So Mercie once againe her selfe displayes,
Out from her sisters cloud, and open layes
Those sunshine lookes, whose beames would dim a thousand dayes.

How may a worme, that crawles along the dust,
Clamber the azure mountaines, thrown so high,
And fetch from thence thy faire Idea just,
That in those sunny courts doth hidden lie,
Cloath'd with such light, as blinds the Angels eye;
How may weake mortall ever hope to file
His unsmooth tongue, and his deprostrate stile?
O raise thou from his corse, thy now entomb'd exile.

One touch would rouze me from my sluggish hearse,
One word would call me to my wished home,
One looke would polish my afflicted verse,
One thought would steale my soule from her thicke lome,
And force it wandring up to heav'n to come,
Thear to importune, and to beg apace
One happy favour of thy sacred grace,
To see, (what though it loose her eyes?) to see thy face.

If any aske why roses please the sight,
Because their leaves upon thy cheekes doe bowre;
If any aske why lillies are so white,
Because their blossoms in thy hand doe flowre:
Or why sweet plants so gratefull odours shoure;
It is because thy breath so like they be:
Or why the Orient Sunne so bright we see;
What reason can we give, but from thine eies, and thee?

Ros'd all in lively crimsin ar thy cheeks,
Whear beawties indeflourishing abide,
And, as to passe his fellowe either seekes,
Seemes both doe blush at one anothers pride:
And on thine eyelids, waiting thee beside,
Ten thousand Graces sit, and when they moove
To earth their amourous belgards from above,
They flie from heav'n, and on their wings convey thy love.

All of discolour'd plumes their wings ar made,
And with so wondrous art the quills ar wrought,
That whensoere they cut the ayrie glade,
The winde into their hollowe pipes is caught:
As seemes the spheres with them they down have brought:
Like to the seaven-fold reede of Arcadie,
Which Pan of Syrinx made, when she did flie
To Ladon sands, and at his sighs sung merily.

As melting hony, dropping from the combe,
So still the words, that spring between thy lipps,
Thy lippes, whear smiling sweetnesse keepes her home,
And heav'nly Eloquence pure manna sipps,
He that his pen but in that fountaine dipps,
How nimbly will the golden phrases flie,
And shed forth streames of choycest rhetorie,
Welling celestiall torrents out of poesie?

Like as the thirstie land, in summers heat,
Calls to the cloudes, and gapes at everie showre,
As though her hungry clifts all heav'n would eat,
Which if high God into her bosome powre,
Though much refresht, yet more she could devoure:
So hang the greedie ears of Angels sweete,
And every breath a thousand cupids meete,
Some flying in, some out, and all about her fleet.

Upon her breast, Delight doth softly sleepe,
And of eternall joy is brought abed,
Those snowie mountelets, through which doe creepe

The milkie rivers, that ar inly bred
In silver cesternes, and themselves doe shed
To wearie Travailers, in heat of day,
To quench their fierie th[ir]st, and to allay
With dropping nectar floods, the furie of their way.

If any wander, thou doest call him backe,
If any be not forward, thou incit'st him,
Thou doest expect, if any should growe slacke,
If any seeme but willing, thou invit'st him,
Or if he doe offend thee, thou acquit'st him,
Thou find'st the lost, and follow'st him that flies,
Healing the sicke, and quickning him that dies,
Thou art the lame mans friendly staffe, the blind mans eyes.

So faire thou art that all would thee behold,
But none can thee behold, thou art so faire,
Pardon, O pardon then thy Vassall bold,
That with poore shadowes strives thee to compare,
And match the things, which he knowes matchlesse are;
O thou vive mirrhour of celestiall grace,
How can fraile colours pourtraict out thy face,
Or paint in flesh thy beawtie, in such semblance base?

Her upper garment was a silken lawne,
With needle-woorke richly embroidered,
Which she her selfe with her owne hand had drawne,
And all the world therein had pourtrayed,
With threads, so fresh, and lively coloured,
That seem'd the world she newe created thear,
And the mistaken eye would rashly swear
The silken trees did growe, and the beasts living wear.

Low at her feet the Earth was cast alone,
(As though to kisse her foot it did aspire,
And gave it selfe for her to tread upon)
With so unlike, and different attire,
That every one that sawe it, did admire
What it might be, was of so various hewe;
For to it selfe it oft so diverse grewe,
That still it seem'd the same, and still it seem'd a newe.

And here, and there few men she scattered,
(That in their thought the world esteeme but small,
And themselves great) but she with one fine thread
So short, and small, and slender wove them all,
That like a sort of busie ants, that crawle
About some molehill, so they wandered:

And round about the waving Sea was shed,
But, for the silver sands, small pearls were sprinkled.

So curiously the underworke did creepe,
And curling circlets so well shadowed lay,
That afar off the waters seem'd to sleepe,
But those that neere the margin pearle did play,
Hoarcely enwaved wear with hastie sway,
As though they meant to rocke the gentle eare,
And hush the former that enslumbred wear,
And here a dangerous rocke the flying ships did fear.

High in the ayrie element there hung
Another clowdy sea, that did disdaine
(As though his purer waves from heaven sprung)
To crawle on earth, as doth the sluggish maine:
But it the earth would water with his raine,
That eb'd, and flow'd, as winde, and season would,
And oft the Sun would cleave the limber mould
To alabaster rockes, that in the liquid rowl'd.

Beneath those sunny banks, a darker cloud,
Dropping with thicker deaw, did melt apace,
And bent it selfe into a hollowe shroude,
On which, if Mercy did but cast her face,
A thousand colours did the bowe enchace,
That wonder was to see the silke distain'd
With the resplendance from her beawtie gain'd,
And Iris paint her locks with beames, so lively feign'd.

About her head a cyprus heav'n she wore,
Spread like a veile, upheld with silver wire,
In which the starres so burn't in golden ore,
As seem'd, the azure web was all on fire,
But hastily, to quench their sparkling ire,
A flood of milke came rowling up the shore,
That on his curded wave swift Argus bore,
And the immortall swan, that did her life deplore.

Yet strange it was, so many starres to see
Without a Sunne, to give their tapers light:
Yet strange it was not, that it so should be:
For, where the Sunne centers himselfe by right,
Her face, and locks did flame, that at the sight,
The heavenly veile, that else should nimbly moove,
Forgot his flight, and all incens'd with love,
With wonder, and amazement, did her beautie proove.

Over her hung a canopie of state,
Not of rich tissew, nor of spangled gold,
But of a substance, though not animate,
Yet of a heav'nly, and spirituall mould,
That onely eyes of Spirits might behold:
Such light as from maine rocks of diamound,
Shooting their sparks at Phebus, would rebound,
And little Angels, holding hands, daunc't all around.

Seemed those little sprights, through nimbless bold,
The stately canopy bore on their wings,
But them it selfe, as pendants, did uphold,
Besides the crownes of many famous kings,
Among the rest, thear David ever sings,
And now, with yeares growne young, renewes his layes
Unto his golden harpe, and ditties playes,
Psalming aloud in well tun'd songs his Makers prayse.

Thou self-Idea of all joyes to come,
Whose love is such, would make the rudest speake,
Whose love is such, would make the wisest dumbe,
O when wilt thou thy too long silence breake,
And overcome the strong to save the weake!
If thou no weapons hast, thine eyes will wound
Th' Almighties selfe, that now sticke on the ground,
As though some blessed object thear did them empound.

Ah miserable Abject of disgrace,
What happines is in thy miserie?
I both must pittie, and envie thy case.
For she, that is the glorie of the skie,
Leaves heaven blind, to fix on thee her eye.
Yet her (though Mercies selfe esteems not small)
The world despis['d], they her Repentance call,
And she her selfe despises, and the world, and all.

Deepely, alas empassioned she stood,
To see a flaming brand, tost up from hell,
Boyling her heart in her owne lustfull blood,
That oft for torment she would loudely yell,
Now she would sighing sit, and nowe she fell
Crouching upon the ground, in sackcloath trust,
Early, and late she prayed, and fast she must,
And all her haire hung full of ashes, and of dust.

Of all most hated, yet hated most of all
Of her owne selfe she was; disconsolat
(As though her flesh did but infunerall

Her buried ghost) she in an arbour sat
Of thornie brier, weeping her cursed state,
And her before a hastie river fled,
Which her blind eyes with faithfull penance fed,
And all about, the grasse with tears hung downe his head.

Her eyes, though blind abroad, at home kept fast,
Inwards they turn'd, and look't into her head,
At which shee often started, as aghast,
To see so fearfull spectacles of dread,
And with one hand, her breast shee martyred,
Wounding her heart, the same to mortifie,
The other a faire damsell held her by,
Which if but once let goe, shee sunke immediatly.

But Faith was quicke, and nimble as the heav'n,
As if of love, and life shee all had been,
And though of present sight her sense were reaven,
Yet shee could see the things could not be seen:
Beyond the starres, as nothing wear between,
She fixt her sight, disdeigning things belowe,
Into the sea she could a mountaine throwe,
And make the Sun to stande, and waters backewards flowe.

Such when as Mercie her beheld from high,
In a darke valley, drownd with her owne tears,
One of her graces she sent hastily,
Smiling Eirene, that a garland wears
Of guilded olive, on her fairer hears,
To crowne the fainting soules true sacrifice,
Whom when as sad Repentance comming spies,
The holy Desperado wip't her swollen eyes.

But Mercie felt a kinde remorse to runne
Through her soft vaines, and therefore, hying fast
To give an end to silence, thus begunne.
Aye-honour'd Father, if no joy thou hast
But to reward desert, reward at last
The Devils voice, spoke with a serpents tongue,
Fit to hisse out the words so deadly stung,
And let him die, deaths bitter charmes so sweetely sung.

He was the father of that hopeles season,
That to serve other Gods, forgot their owne,
The reason was, thou wast above their reason:
They would have any Gods, rather then none,
A beastly serpent, or a senselesse stone:
And these, as Justice hates, so I deplore:

But the up-plowed heart, all rent, and tore,
Though wounded by it selfe, I gladly would restore.

He was but dust; Why fear'd he not to fall?
And beeing fall'n, how can he hope to live?
Cannot the hand destroy him, that made all?
Could he not take away, aswell as give?
Should man deprave, and should not God deprive?
Was it not all the worlds deceiving spirit,
(That, bladder'd up with pride of his owne merit,
Fell in his rise) that him of heav'n did disinherit?

He was but dust: how could he stand before him?
And beeing fall'n, why should he feare to die?
Cannot the hand that made him first, restore him?
Deprav'd of sinne, should he deprived lie
Of grace? can he not hide infirmitie
That gave him strength? unworthy the forsaking,
He is, who ever weighs, without mistaking,
Or Maker of the man, or manner of his making.

Who shall thy temple incense any more;
Or to thy altar crowne the sacrifice;
Or strewe with idle flow'rs the hallow'd flore;
Or what should Prayer deck with hearbs, and spice,
Her vialls, breathing orisons of price?
If all must paie that which all cannot paie?
O first begin with mee, and Mercie slaie,
And thy thrice-honour'd Sonne, that now beneath doth strey.

But if or he, or I may live, and speake,
And heav'n can joye to see a sinner weepe,
Oh let not Justice yron scepter breake
A heart alreadie broke, that lowe doth creep,
And with prone humblesse her feets dust doth sweep.
Must all goe by desert? is nothing free?
Ah, if but those that onely woorthy be,
None should thee ever see, none should thee ever see.

What hath man done, that man shall not undoe,
Since God to him is growne so neere a kin?
Did his foe slay him? he shall slay his foe:
Hath he lost all? he all againe shall win;
Is Sinne his Master? he shall master sinne:
Too hardy soule, with sinne the field to trie:
The onely way to conquer, was to flie,
But thus long death hath liv'd, and now deaths selfe shall die.

He is a path, if any be misled,
He is a robe, if any naked bee,
If any chaunce to hunger, he is bread,
If any be a bondman, he is free,
If any be but weake, howe strong is hee?
To dead men life he is, to sicke men health,
To blinde men sight, and to the needie wealth,
A pleasure without losse, a treasure without stealth.

Who can forget, never to be forgot,
The time, that all the world in slumber lies,
When, like the starres, the singing Angels shot
To earth, and heav'n awaked all his eyes,
To see another Sunne, at midnight rise,
On ear[t]h? was never sight of pareil fame,
For God before Man like himselfe did frame,
But God himselfe now like a mortall man became.

A Child he was, and had not learn't to speake,
That with his word the world before did make,
His Mothers armes him bore, he was so weake,
That with one hand the vaults of heav'n could shake,
See how small roome my infant Lord doth take,
Whom all the world is not enough to hold.
Who of his yeares, or of his age hath told?
Never such age so young, never a child so old.

And yet but newely he was infanted,
And yet alreadie he was sought to die,
Yet scarcely borne, alreadie banished,
Not able yet to goe, and forc't to flie,
But scarcely fled away, when by and by,
The Tyrans sword with blood is all defil'd,
And Rachel, for her sonnes with furie wild,
Cries, O thou cruell King, and O my sweetest child.

Egypt his Nource became, whear Nilus springs,
Who streit, to entertaine the rising sunne,
The hasty harvest in his bosome brings;
But now for drieth the fields wear all undone,
And now with waters all is overrunne,
So fast the Cynthian mountaines powr'd their snowe,
When once they felt the sunne so neere them glowe,
That Nilus Egypt lost, and to a sea did growe.

The Angells caroll'd lowd their song of peace,
The cursed Oracles wear strucken dumb,
To see their Sheapheard, the poore Sheapheards press,

To see their King, the Kingly Sophies come,
And them to guide unto his Masters home,
A Starre comes dauncing up the orient,
That springs for joye over the strawy tent,
Whear gold, to make their Prince a crowne, they all present.

Young John, glad child, before he could be borne,
Leapt in the woombe, his joy to prophecie,
Old Anna though with age all spent, and worne,
Proclaimes her Saviour to posteritie,
And Simeon fast his dying notes doeth plie.
Oh how the blessed soules about him trace.
It is the fire of heav'n thou doest embrace,
Sing, Simeon, sing, sing Simeon, sing apace.

With that the mightie thunder dropt away
From Gods unwarie arme, now milder growne,
And melted into teares, as if to pray
For pardon, and for pittie, it had knowne,
That should have been for sacred vengeance throwne:
Thereto the Armies Angelique dev[ow'd]
Their former rage, and all to Mercie b[ow'd],
Their broken weapons at her feet they gladly strow'd.

Bring, bring ye Graces all your silver flaskets,
Painted with every choicest flowre that growes,
That I may soone unflow'r your fragrant baskets,
To strowe the fields with odours whear he goes,
Let what so e're he treads on be a rose.
So downe shee let her eyelids fall, to shine
Upon the rivers of bright Palestine,
Whose woods drop honie, and her rivers skip with wine.

CANTO II

But now the second Morning, from her bowre,
Began to glister in her beames, and nowe
The roses of the day began to flowre
In th' easterne garden; for heav'ns smiling browe
Halfe insolent for joy begunne to showe:
The early Sunne came lively dauncing out,
And the bragge lambes ranne wantoning about,
That heav'n, and earth might seeme in tryumph both to shout.

Th' engladded Spring, forgetfull now to weepe,
Began t' eblazon from her leavie bed,

The waking swallowe broke her halfe-yeares sleepe,
And everie bush lay deepely purpured
With violets, the woods late-wintry head
Wide flaming primroses set all on fire,
And his bald trees put on their greene attire,
Among whose infant leaves the joyeous birds conspire.

And now the taller Sonnes (whom Titan warmes)
Of unshorne mountaines, blowne with easie windes,
Dandled the mornings childhood in their armes,
And, if they chaunc't to slip the prouder pines,
The under Corylets did catch the shines,
To guild their leaves, sawe never happie yeare
Such joyfull triumph, and triumphant cheare,
As though the aged world anew created wear.

Say Earth, why hast thou got thee new attire,
And stick'st thy habit full of dazies red?
Seems that thou doest to some high thought aspire,
And some newe-found-out Bridegroome mean'st to wed:
Tell me ye Trees, so fresh apparelled,
So never let the spitefull Canker wast you,
So never let the heav'ns with lightening blast you,
Why goe you now so trimly drest, or whither hast you?

Answer me Jordan, why thy crooked tide
So often wanders from his neerest way,
As though some other way thy streame would slide,
And faine salute the place where something lay?
And you sweete birds, that shaded from the ray,
Sit carolling, and piping griefe away,
The while the lambs to heare you daunce, and play,
Tell me sweete birds, what is it you so faine would say?

And, thou faire Spouse of Earth, that everie yeare,
Gett'st such a numerous issue of thy bride,
How chance thou hotter shin'st, and draw'st more neere?
Sure thou somewhear some worthie sight hast spide,
That in one place for joy thou canst not bide:
And you dead Swallowes, that so lively now
Through the flit aire your winged passage rowe,
How could new life into your frozen ashes flowe?

Ye Primroses, and purple violets,
Tell me, why blaze ye from your leavie bed,
And wooe mens hands to rent you from your sets,
As though you would somewhear be carried,
With fresh perfumes, and velvets garnished?

But ah, I neede not aske, 'tis surely so,
You all would to your Saviours triumphs goe,
Thear would ye all awaite, and humble homage doe.

Thear should the Earth herselfe with garlands newe
And lovely flo[w'r]s embellished adore,
Such roses never in her garland grewe,
Such lillies never in her brest she wore,
Like beautie never yet did shine before:
Thear should the Sunne another Sunne behold,
From whence himselfe borrowes his locks of gold,
That kindle heav'n, and earth with beauties manifold.

Thear might the violet, and primrose sweet
Beames of more lively, and more lovely grace,
Arising from their beds of incense meet;
Thear should the Swallowe see newe life embrace
Dead ashes, and the grave unheale his face,
To let the living from his bowels creepe,
Unable longer his owne dead to keepe:
Thear heav'n, and earth should see their Lord awake from sleepe.

Their Lord, before by other judg'd to die,
Nowe Judge of all himselfe, before forsaken
Of all the world, that from his aide did flie,
Now by the Saints into their armies taken,
Before for an unworthie man mistaken,
Nowe worthy to be God confest, before
With blasphemies by all the basest tore,
Now worshipped by Angels, that him lowe adore.

Whose garment was before indipt in blood,
But now, imbright'ned into heav'nly flame,
The Sun it selfe outglitters, though he should
Climbe to the toppe of the celestiall frame,
And force the starres go hide themselves for shame:
Before that under earth was buried,
But nowe about the heav'ns is carried,
And thear for ever by the Angels heried.

So fairest Phosphor the bright Morning starre,
But neewely washt in the greene element,
Before the drouzie Night is halfe aware,
Shooting his flaming locks with deaw besprent,
Springs lively up into the orient,
And the bright drove, fleec't all in gold, he chaces
To drinke, that on the Olympique mountaine grazes,
The while the minor Planets forfeit all their faces.

So long he wandred in our lower spheare,
That heav'n began his cloudy starres despise,
Halfe envious, to see on earth appeare
A greater light, then flam'd in his owne skies:
At length it burst for spight, and out thear flies
A globe of winged Angels, swift as thought,
That, on their spotted feathers, lively caught
The sparkling Earth, and to their azure fields it brought.

The rest, that yet amazed stood belowe,
With eyes cast up, as greedie to be fed,
And hands upheld, themselves to ground did throwe,
So when the Trojan boy was ravished,
As through th' Idalian woods they saie he fled,
His aged Gardians stood all dismai'd,
Some least he should have fallen back afraid,
And some their hasty vowes, and timely prayers said.

Tosse up your heads ye everlasting gates,
And let the Prince of glorie enter in:
At whose brave voly of sideriall States,
The Sunne to blush, and starres growe pale wear seene,
When, leaping first from earth, he did begin
To climbe his Angells wings; then open hang
Your christall doores, so all the chorus sang
Of heav'nly birds, as to the starres they nimbly sprang.

Hearke how the floods clap their applauding hands,
The pleasant valleyes singing for delight,
And wanton Mountaines daunce about the Lands,
The while the fieldes, struck with the heav'nly light,
Set all their flo[w'r]s a smiling at the sight,
The trees laugh with their blossoms, and the sound
Of the triumphant shout of praise, that crown'd
The flaming Lambe, breaking through heav'n, hath passage found.

Out leap the antique Patriarchs, all in hast,
To see the po[w'r]s of Hell in triumph lead,
And with small starres a garland interchast
Of olive leaves they bore, to crowne his head,
That was before with thornes degloried,
After them flewe the Prophets, brightly stol'd
In shining lawne, and wimpled manifold,
Striking their yvorie harpes, strung all in chords of gold.

To which the Saints victorious carolls sung,
Ten thousand Saints at once, that with the sound,

The hollow vaults of heav'n for triumph rung:
The Cherubins their clamours did confound
With all the rest, and clapt their wings around:
Downe from their thrones the Dominations flowe,
And at his feet their crownes, and scepters throwe,
And all the princely Soules fell on their faces lowe.

Nor can the Martyrs wounds them stay behind,
But out they rush among the heav'nly crowd,
Seeking their heav'n out of their heav'n to find,
Sounding their silver trumpets out so loude,
That the shrill noise broke through the starrie cloude,
And all the virgin Soules, in pure araie,
Came dauncing forth, and making joyeous plaie;
So him they lead along into the courts of day.

So him they lead into the courts of day,
Whear never warre, nor wounds abide him more,
But in that house, eternall peace doth plaie,
Acquieting the soules, that newe before
Their way to heav'n through their owne blood did skore,
But now, estranged from all miserie,
As farre as heav'n, and earth discoasted lie,
Swelter in quiet waves of immortalitie.

And if great things by smaller may be ghuest,
So, in the mid'st of Neptunes angrie tide,
Our Britan Island, like the weedie nest
Of true Halcyon, on the waves doth ride,
And softly sayling, skornes the waters pride:
While all the rest, drown'd on the continent,
And tost in bloodie waves, their wounds lament,
And stand, to see our peace, as struck with woonderment.

The Ship of France religious waves doe tosse,
And Greec[e] it selfe is now growne barbarous,
Spains Children hardly dare the Ocean crosse,
And Belges field lies wast, and ruinous,
That unto those, the heav'ns ar invious,
And unto them, themselves ar strangers growne,
And unto these, the Seas ar faithles knowne,
And unto her, alas, her owne is not her owne.

Here onely shut we Janus yron gates,
And call the welcome Muses to our springs,
And ar but Pilgrims from our heav'nly states,
The while the trusty Earth sure plentie brings,
And Ships through Neptune safely spread their wings.

Goe blessed Island, wander wheare thou please,
Unto thy God, or men, heav'n, lands, or seas,
Thou canst not loose thy way, thy King with all hath peace.

Deere Prince, thy Subjects joy, hope of their heirs,
Picture of peace, or breathing Image rather,
The certaine argument of all our pray'rs,
Thy Harries, and thy Countries lovely Father,
Let Peace, in endles joyes, for ever bath her
Within thy sacred brest, that at thy birth
Brought'st her with thee from heav'n, to dwell on earth,
Making our earth a heav'n, and paradise of mirth.

Let not my Liege misdeem these humble laies,
As lick't with soft, and supple blandishment,
Or spoken to disparagon his praise;
For though pale Cynthia, neere her brothers tent,
Soone disappeares in the white firmament,
And gives him back the beames, before wear his,
Yet when he verges, or is hardly ris,
She the vive image of her absent brother is.

Nor let the Prince of peace his beadsman blame,
That with his Stewart dares his Lord compare,
And heav'nly peace with earthly quiet shame:
So Pines to lowely plants compared ar,
And lightning Phoebus to a little starre:
And well I wot, my rime, albee unsmooth,
Ne, saies but what it meanes, ne meanes but sooth,
Ne harmes the good, ne good to harmefull person doth.

Gaze but upon the house, wheare Man embo[w'r]s:
With flo[w'r]s, and rushes paved is his way,
Wheare all the Creatures ar his Servitours,
The windes doe sweepe his chambers every day,
And cloudes doe wash his rooms, the seeling gay,
Starred aloft the guilded knobs embrave:
If such a house God to another gave,
How shine those glittering courts, he for himselfe will have?

And if a sullen cloud, as sad as night,
In which the Sunne may seeme embodied,
Depur'd of all his drosse, we see so white,
Burning in melted gold his watrie head,
Or round with yvorie edges silvered,
What lustre superexcellent will he
Lighten on those, that shall his sunneshine see,
In that all-glorious court, in which all glories be

If but one Sunne, with his diffusive fires,
Can paint the starres, and the whole world with light,
And joy, and life into each heart inspires,
And every Saint shall shine in heav'n, as bright
As doth the Sunne in his transcendent might,
(As faith may well beleeve, what Truth once sayes)
What shall so many Sunnes united rayes
But dazle all the eyes, that nowe in heav'n we praise?

Here let my Lord hang up his conquering launce,
And bloody armour with late slaughter warme,
And looking downe on his weake Militants,
Behold his Saints, mid'st of their hot alarme,
Hang all their golden hopes upon his arme.
And in this lower field dispacing wide,
Through windie thoughts, that would thei[r] sayles misguide,
Anchor their fleshly ships fast in his wounded side.

Here may the Band, that now in Tryumph shines,
And that (before they wear invested thus)
In earthly bodies carried heavenly mindes,
Pitcht round about in order glorious,
Their sunny Tents, and houses luminous,
All their eternall day in songs employing,
Joying their ende, without ende of their joying,
While their almightie Prince Destruction is destroying.

Full, yet without satietie, of that
Which whetts, and quiets greedy Appetite,
Whear never Sunne did rise, nor ever sat,
But one eternall day, and endles light
Gives time to those, whose time is infinite,
Speaking with thought, obtaining without fee,
Beholding him, whom never eye could see,
And magnifying him, that cannot greater be.

How can such joy as this want words to speake?
And yet what words can speake such joy as this?
Far from the world, that might their quiet breake,
Here the glad Soules the face of beauty kisse,
Powr'd out in pleasure, on their beds of blisse.
And drunke with nectar torrents, ever hold
Their eyes on him, whose graces manifold,
The more they doe behold, the more they would behold.

Their sight drinkes lovely fires in at their eyes,
Their braine sweete incense with fine breath accloyes,

That on Gods sweating altar burning lies,
Their hungrie cares feede on their heav'nly noyse,
That Angels sing, to tell their untould joyes;
Their understanding naked Truth, their wills
The all, and selfe-sufficient Goodnesse fills,
That nothing here is wanting, but the want of ills.

No Sorrowe nowe hangs clowding on their browe,
No bloodles Maladie empales their face,
No Age drops on their hayrs his silver snowe,
No Nakednesse their bodies doeth embase,
No Povertie themselves, and theirs disgrace,
No feare of death the joy of life devours,
No unchast sleepe their precious time deflowrs,
No losse, no griefe, no change waite on their winged hour's.

But now their naked bodies skorne the cold,
And from their eyes joy lookes, and laughs at paine,
The Infant wonders how he came so old,
And old man how he came so young againe;
Still resting, though from sleepe they still refraine,
Whear all are rich, and yet no gold they owe,
And all are Kings, and yet no Subjects knowe,
All full, and yet no time on foode they doe bestowe.

For things that passe are past, and in this field,
The indeficient Spring no Winter feares,
The Trees together fruit, and blossome yeild,
Th' unfading Lilly leaves of silver beares,
And crimson rose a skarlet garment weares:
And all of these on the Saints bodies growe,
Not, as they woont, on baser earth belowe;
Three rivers heer of milke, and wine, and honie flowe.

About the holy Cittie rowles a flood
Of moulten chrystall, like a sea of glasse,
On which weake streame a strong foundation stood,
Of living Diamounds the building was,
That all things else, besides it selfe, did passe.
Her streetes, in stead of stones, the starres did pave,
And little pearles, for dust, it seem'd to have,
On which soft-streaming Manna, like pure snowe, did wave.

In mid'st of this Citie coelestiall,
Whear the eternall Temple should have rose,
Light'ned th' Idea Beatificall:
End, and beginning of each thing that growes,
Whose selfe no end, nor yet beginning knowes,

That hath no eyes to see, nor ears to heare,
Yet sees, and heares, and is all-eye, all-eare,
That no whear is contain'd, and yet is every whear.

Changer of all things, yet immutable,
Before, and after all, the first, and last,
That mooving all, is yet immoveable,
Great without quantitie, in whose forecast,
Things past are present, things to come are past,
Swift without motion, to whose open eye
The hearts of wicked men unbrested lie,
At once absent, and present to them, farre, and nigh.

It is no flaming lustre, made of light,
No sweet concent, or well-tim'd harmonie,
Ambrosia, for to feast the Appetite,
Or flowrie odour, mixt with spicerie.
No soft embrace, or pleasure bodily,
And yet it is a kinde of inward feast,
A harmony, that sounds within the brest,
An odour, light, embrace, in which the soule doth rest.

A heav'nly feast, no hunger can consume,
A light unseene, yet shines in every place,
A sound, no time can steale, a sweet perfume,
No windes can scatter, an intire embrace,
That no satietie can ere unlace,
Ingrac't into so high a favour, thear
The Saints, with their Beaw-peers, whole worlds outwear,
And things unseene doe see, and things unheard doe hear.

Ye blessed soules, growne richer by your spoile,
Whose losse, though great, is cause of greater gaines,
Here may your weary Spirits rest from toyle,
Spending your endlesse eav'ning, that remaines,
Among those white flocks, and celestiall traines,
That feed upon their Sheapheards eyes, and frame
That heav'nly musique of so woondrous fame,
Psalming aloude the holy honours of his name.

Had I a voice of steel to tune my song,
Wear every verse as smoothly fil'd as glasse,
And every member turned to a tongue,
And every tongue wear made of sounding brasse,
Yet all that skill, and all this strength, alas,
Should it presume to guild, wear misadvis'd,
The place, whear David hath new songs devis'd,
As in his burning throne he sits emparadis'd.

Most happie Prince, whose eyes those starres behould,
Treading ours under feet, now maist thou powre
That overflowing skill, whearwith of ould
Thou woont'st to combe rough speech, now maist thou showr
Fresh streames of praise upon that holy bowre,
Which well we heaven call, not that it rowles,
But that it is the haven of our soules.
Most happie Prince, whose sight so heav'nly sight behoulds.

Ah foolish Sheapheards, that wear woont esteem,
Your God all rough, and shaggy-hair'd to bee;
And yet farre wiser Sheapheards then ye deeme,
For who so poore (though who so rich) as hee,
When, with us hermiting in lowe degree,
He wash't his flocks in Jordans spotles tide,
And, that his deere remembrance aie might bide,
Did to us come, and with us liv'd, and for us di'd?

But now so lively colours did embeame
His sparkling forehead, and so shiny rayes
Kindled his flaming locks; that downe did streame
In curles, along his necke, whear sweetly playes
(Singing his wounds of love in sacred layes)
His deerest Spouse, Spouse of the deerest Lover,
Knitting a thousand knots over, and over,
And dying still for love, but they her still recover.

Faire Egliset, that at his eyes doth dresse
Her glorious face, those eyes, from whence ar shed
Infinite belamours, whear to expresse
His love, high God all heav'n as captive leads,
And all the banners of his grace dispreads,
And in those windowes, doth his armes englaze,
And on those eyes, the Angels all doe gaze,
And from those eies, the lights of heav'n do gleane their blaze.

But let the Kentish lad, that lately taught
His oaten reed the trumpets silver sound,
Young Thyrsilis, and for his musique brought
The willing sphears from heav'n, to lead a round
Of daunceing Nymphs, and Heards, that sung, and crown'd
Eclectas hymen with ten thousand flowrs
Of choycest prayse, and hung her heav'nly bow'rs
With saffron garlands, drest for Nuptiall Paramours,

Let his shrill trumpet, with her silver blast,
Of faire Eclecta, and her Spousall bed,

Be the sweet pipe, and smooth Encomiast:
But my greene Muse, hiding her younger head
Under old Chamus flaggy banks, that spread
Their willough locks abroad, and all the day
With their owne watry shadowes wanton play,
Dares not those high amours, and love-sick songs assay.

Impotent words, weake sides, that strive in vaine,
In vaine, alas, to tell so heav'nly sight,
So heav'nly sight, as none can greater feigne,
Feigne what he can, that seemes of greatest might,
Might any yet compare with Infinite?
Infinite sure those joyes, my words but light,
Light is the pallace whear she dwells. O blessed wight!

CANTO III

So downe the silver streames of Eridan,
On either side bank't with a lilly wall,
Whiter then both, rides the triumphant Swan,
And sings his dirge, and prophesies his fall,
Diving into his watrie funerall:
But Eridan to Cedron must submit
His flowry shore, nor can he envie it,
If when Apollo sings, his swans doe silent sit.

That heav'nly voice I more delight to heare,
Then gentle ayres to breath, or swelling waves
Against the sounding rocks their bosomes teare,
Or whistling reeds, that rutty Jordan laves,
And with their verdure his white head embraves,
To chide the windes, or hiving bees, that flie
About the laughing bloosms of sallowie,
Rocking asleepe the idle groomes that lazie lie.

And yet, how can I heare thee singing goe,
When men incens'd with hate, thy death foreset?
Or els, why doe I heare thee sighing so,
When thou, inflam'd with love, their life doest get?
That Love, and hate, and sighs, and songs are met;
But thus, and onely thus thy love did crave,
To sende thee singing for us to thy grave,
While we sought thee to kill, and thou sought'st us to save.

When I remember Christ our burden beares,
I looke for glorie, but finde miserie;
I looke for joy, but finde a sea of teares;

I looke that we should live, and finde him die;
I looke for Angels songs, and heare him crie:
Thus what I looke, I cannot finde so well,
Or rather, what I finde, I cannot tell,
These bankes so narrowe are, those streames so highly swell.

Christ suffers, and in this, his teares begin,
Suffers for us, and our joy springs in this,
Suffers to death, here is his Manhood seen,
Suffers to rise, and here his Godhead is.
For Man, that could not by himselfe have ris,
Out of the grave doth by the Godhead rise,
And God, that could not die, in Manhood dies,
That we in both might live, by that sweete sacrifice.

Goe giddy braines, whose witts are thought so fresh,
Plucke all the flo[w'r]s that Nature forth doth throwe,
Goe sticke them on the cheekes of wanton flesh;
Poore idol, (forc't at once to fall and growe)
Of fading roses, and of melting snowe:
Your songs exceede your matter, this of mine,
The matter, which it sings, shall make divine,
As starres dull puddles guild, in which their beauties shine.

Who doth not see drown'd in Deucalions name,
(When earth his men, and sea had lost his shore)
Old Noah; and in Nisus lock, the fame
Of Sampson yet alive; and long before
In Phaethons, mine owne fall I deplore:
But he that conquer'd hell, to fetch againe
His virgin widowe, by a serpent slaine,
Another Orpheus was then dreaming poets feigne.

That taught the stones to melt for passion,
And dormant sea, to heare him, silent lie,
And at his voice, the watrie nation
To flocke, as if they deem'd it cheape, to buy
With their owne deaths his sacred harmonie:
The while the waves stood still to heare his song,
And steadie shore wav'd with the reeling throng
Of thirstie soules, that hung upon his fluent tongue.

What better friendship, then to cover shame?
What greater love, then for a friend to die?
Yet this is better to asself the blame,
And this is greater, for an enemie:
But more then this, to die, not suddenly,
Not with some common death, or easie paine,

But slowely, and with torments to be slaine,
O depth, without a depth, farre better seene, then saine!

And yet the Sonne is humbled for the Slave,
And yet the Slave is proude before the Sonne:
Yet the Creator for his creature gave
Himselfe, and yet the creature hasts to runne
From his Creator, and self-good doth shunne:
And yet the Prince, and God himselfe doth crie
To Man, his Traitour, pardon not to flie,
Yet Man his God, and Traytour doth his Prince defie.

Who is it sees not that he nothing is,
But he that nothing sees; what weaker brest,
Since Adams Armour fail'd, dares warrant his?
That made by God of all his creatures best,
Strait made himselfe the woorst of all the rest:
"If any strength we have, it is to ill,
But all the good is Gods, both pow'r, and will":
The dead man cannot rise, though he himselfe may kill.

But let the thorny schools these punctualls
Of wills, all good, or bad, or neuter diss;
Such joy we gained by our parentalls,
That good, or bad, whither I cannot wiss,
To call it a mishap, or happy miss
That fell from Eden, and to heav'n did rise:
Albee the mitred Card'nall more did prize
His part in Paris, then his part in Paradise.

A Tree was first the instrument of strife,
Whear Eve to sinne her soule did prostitute,
A Tree is now the instrument of life,
Though ill that trunke, and this faire body suit:
Ah, cursed tree, and yet O blessed fruit!
That death to him, this life to us doth give:
Strange is the cure, when things past cure revive,
And the Physitian dies, to make his patient live.

Sweete Eden was the arbour of delight,
Yet in his hony flo[w'r]s our poyson blew;
Sad Gethseman the bowre of balefull night,
Whear Christ a health of poison for us drewe,
Yet all our hony in that poyson grewe:
So we from sweetest flo[w'r]s, could sucke our bane,
And Christ from bitter venome, could againe
Extract life out of death, and pleasure out of paine.

A Man was first the author of our fall,
A Man is now the author of our rise,
A Garden was the place we perisht all,
A Garden is the place he payes our price,
And the old Serpent with a newe devise,
Hath found a way himselfe for to beguile,
So he, that all men tangled in his wile,
Is now by one man caught, beguil'd with his owne guile.

The dewie night had with her frostie shade
Immant'led all the world, and the stiffe ground
Sparkled in yce, onely the Lord, that made
All for himselfe, himselfe dissolved found,
Sweat without heat, and bled without a wound:
Of heav'n, and earth, and God, and Man forlore,
Thrice begging helpe of those, whose sinnes he bore,
And thrice denied of those, not to denie had swore.

Yet had he beene alone of God forsaken,
Or had his bodie beene imbroyl'd alone
In fierce assault, he might, perhaps, have taken
Some joy in soule, when all joy els was gone,
But that with God, and God to heav'n is flow'n;
And Hell it selfe out from her grave doth rise,
Black as the starles night, and with them flies,
Yet blacker then they both, the Sonne of blasphemies.

As when the Planets, with unkind aspect,
Call from her caves the meager pestilence,
The sacred vapour, eager to infect,
Obeyes the voyce of the sad influence,
And vomits up a thousand noysome sents,
The well of life, flaming his golden flood
With the sicke ayre, fevers the boyling blood,
And poisons all the bodie with contagious food.

The bold Physitian, too incautelous,
By those he cures, himselfe is murdered,
Kindnes infects, pitie is dangerous,
And the poore infant, yet not fully bred,
Thear where he should be borne, lies buried:
So the darke Prince, from his infernall cell,
Casts up his griesly Torturers of hell,
And whets them to revenge, with his insulting spell.

See how the world smiles in eternall peace;
While we, the harmles brats, and rustie throng
Of Night, our snakes in curles doe pranke, and dresse:

Why sleepe our drouzie scorpions so long?
Whear is our wonted vertue to doe wrong?
Are we our selves; or are we Graces growen?
The Sonnes of hell, or heav'n? was never knowne
Our whips so over-moss't, and brands so deadly blowne.

O long desired, never hop't for howre,
When our Tormentour shall our torments feele!
Arme, arme your selves, sad Dires of my pow'r,
And make our Judge for pardon to us kneele,
Slise, launch, dig, teare him with your whips of steele:
My selfe in honour of so noble prize,
Will powre you reaking blood, shed with the cries
Of hastie heyres, who their owne fathers sacrifice.

With that a flood of poyson, blacke as hell,
Out from his filthy gorge, the beast did spue,
That all about his blessed bodie fell,
And thousand flaming serpents hissing flew
About his soule, from hellish sulphur threw,
And every one brandisht his fierie tongue,
And woorming all about his soule they clung,
But he their stings tore out, and to the ground them flung.

So have I seene a rocks heroique brest,
Against proud Neptune, that his ruin threats,
When all his waves he hath to battle prest,
And with a thousand swelling billows beats
The stubborne stone, and foams, and chafes, and frets
To heave him from his root, unmooved stand;
And more in heapes the barking surges band,
The more in pieces beat, flie weeping to the strand.

So may wee oft a vent'rous father see,
To please his wanton sonne, his onely joy,
Coast all about, to catch the roving bee,
And stung himselfe, his busie hands employ
To save the honie, for the gamesome boy:
Or from the snake her rank'rous teeth erace,
Making his child the toothles Serpent chace,
Or, with his little hands, her tum'rous gorge embrace.

Thus Christ himselfe to watch, and sorrow gives,
While, deaw'd in easie sleepe, dead Peter lies:
Thus Man in his owne grave securely lives,
While Christ alive, with thousand horrours dies,
Yet more for theirs, then his owne pardon cries:
No sinnes he had, yet all our sinnes he bare,

So much doth God for others evills care,
And yet so careles men for their owne evills are.

See drouzie Peter, see whear Judas wakes,
Whear Judas kisses him whom Peter flies:
O kisse more deadly then the sting of snakes!
False love more hurtfull then true injuries!
Aye me! how deerly God his Servant buies?
For God his man, at his owne blood doth hold,
And Man his God, for thirtie pence hath sold.
So tinne for silver goes, and dunghill drosse for gold.

Yet was it not enough for Sinne to chuse
A Servant, to betray his Lord to them;
But that a Subject must his King accuse,
But that a Pagan must his God condemne,
But that a Father must his Sonne contemne,
But that the Sonne must his owne death desire,
That Prince, and People, Servant, and the Sire,
Gentil, and Jewe, and he against himselfe conspire?

Was this the oyle, to make thy Saints adore thee,
The froathy spittle of the rascall throng?
Ar these the virges, that ar borne before thee,
Base whipps of corde, and knotted all along?
Is this thy golden scepter, against wrong,
A reedie cane? is that the crowne adornes
Thy shining locks, a crowne of spiny thornes?
Ar theas the Angels himns, the Priests blasphemous scornes?

Who ever sawe Honour before asham'd;
Afflicted Majestie, debased height;
Innocence guiltie, Honestie defam'd;
Libertie bound, Health sick, the Sunne in night?
But since such wrong was offred unto right,
Our night is day, our sicknes health is growne,
Our shame is veild, this now remaines alone
For us, since he was ours, that wee bee not our owne.

Night was ordeyn'd for rest, and not for paine,
But they, to paine their Lord, their rest contemne,
Good lawes to save, what bad men would have slaine,
And not bad Judges, with one breath, by them
The innocent to pardon, and condemne:
Death for revenge of murderers, not decaie
Of guiltles blood, but now, all headlong sway
Mans Murderer to save, mans Saviour to slaie.

Fraile Multitude, whose giddy lawe is list,
And best applause is windy flattering,
Most like the breath of which it doth consist,
No sooner blowne, but as soone vanishing,
As much desir'd, as little profiting,
That makes the men that have it oft as light,
As those that give it, which the proud invite,
And feare: the bad mans friend, the good mans hypocrite.

It was but now their sounding clamours sung,
Blessed is he, that comes from the most high,
And all the mountaines with Hosanna rung,
And nowe, away with him, away they crie,
And nothing can be heard but crucifie:
It was but now, the Crowne it selfe they save,
And golden name of King unto him gave,
And nowe, no King, but onely Caesar, they will have:

It was but now they gathered blooming May,
And of his armes disrob'd the branching tree,
To strowe with boughs, and blossomes all thy way,
And now, the branchlesse truncke a crosse for thee,
And May, dismai'd, thy coronet must be:
It was but now they wear so kind, to throwe
Their owne best garments, whear thy feet should goe,
And now, thy selfe they strip, and bleeding wounds they show.

See whear the author of all life is dying:
O fearefull day! he dead, what hope of living?
See whear the hopes of all our lives are buying:
O chearfull day! they bought, what feare of grieving?
Love love for hate, and death for life is giving:
Loe how his armes are stretch't abroad to grace thee,
And, as they open stand, call to embrace thee,
Why stai'st thou then my soule; O flie, flie thither hast thee.

His radious head, with shamefull thornes they teare,
His tender backe, with bloody whipps they rent,
His side and heart, they furrowe with a spear,
His hands, and feete, with riving nayles they tent,
And, as to disentrayle his soule they meant,
They jolly at his griefe, and make their game,
His naked body to expose to shame,
That all might come to see, and all might see, that came.

Whereat the heav'n put out his guiltie eye,
That durst behold so execrable sight,
And sabled all in blacke the shadie skie,

And the pale starres strucke with unwonted fright,
Quenched their everlasting lamps in night:
And at his birth as all the starres heav'n had,
Wear not enough, but a newe star was made,
So now both newe, and old, and all away did fade.

The mazed Angels shooke their fierie wings,
Readie to lighten vengeance from Gods throne,
One downe his eyes upon the Manhood flings,
Another gazes on the Godhead, none
But surely thought his wits wear not his owne:
Some flew, to looke if it wear very hee,
But, when Gods arme unarmed they did see,
Albee they sawe it was, they vow'd it could not bee.

The sadded aire hung all in cheerelesse blacke,
Through which, the gentle windes soft sighing flewe,
And Jordan into such huge sorrowe brake,
(As if his holy streame no measure knewe,)
That all his narrowe bankes he overthrewe,
The trembling earth with horrour inly shooke,
And stubborne stones, such griefe unus'd to brooke,
Did burst, and ghosts awaking from their graves gan looke.

The wise Philosopher cried, all agast,
The God of nature surely lanquished,
The sad Centurion cried out as fast,
The Sonne of God, the Sonne of God was dead,
The headlong Jew hung downe his pensive head,
And homewards far'd, and ever, as he went,
He smote his brest, halfe desperately bent,
The verie woods, and beasts did seeme his death lament.

The gracelesse Traytour round about did looke,
(He lok't not long, the Devill quickely met him)
To finde a halter, which he found, and tooke,
Onely a gibbet nowe he needes must get him,
So on a wither'd tree he fairly set him,
And helpt him fit the rope, and in his thought
A thousand furies, with their whippes, he brought,
So thear he stands, readie to hell to make his vault.

For him a waking bloodhound, yelling loude,
That in his bosome long had sleeping layde,
A guiltie Conscience, barking after blood,
Pursued eagerly, ne ever stai'd,
Till the betrayers selfe it had betray'd.
Oft chang'd he place, in hope away to winde,

But change of place could never change his minde,
Himselfe he flies to loose, and followes for to finde.

Thear is but two wayes for this soule to have,
When parting from the body, forth it purges,
To flie to heav'n, or fall into the grave,
Where whippes of scorpions, with the stinging scourges,
Feed on the howling ghosts, and firie Surges
Of brimstone rowle about the cave of night,
Where flames doe burne, and yet no sparke of light,
And fire both fries, and freezes the blaspheming spright.

Thear lies the captive soule, aye-sighing sore,
Reck'ning a thousand yeares since her first bands,
Yet staies not thear, but addes a thousand more,
And at another thousand never stands,
But tells to them the starres, and heapes the sands,
And now the starres are told, and sands are runne,
And all those thousand thousand myriads done,
And yet but now, alas! but now all is begunne.

With that a flaming brand a Furie catch't,
And shooke, and tost it round in his wilde thought,
So from his heart all joy, all comfort snatch't,
With every starre of hope, and as he sought,
(With present feare, and future griefe distraught)
To flie from his owne heart, and aide implore
Of him, the more he gives, that hath the more,
Whose storehouse is the heavens, too little for his store.

Stay wretch on earth, cried Satan, restles rest,
Know'st thou not Justice lives in heav'n; or can
The worst of creatures live among the best;
Among the blessed Angels cursed man?
Will Judas now become a Christian?
Whither will hopes long wings transport thy minde;
Or canst thou not thy selfe a sinner finde;
Or cruell to thy selfe, wouldst thou have Mercie kinde?

He gave thee life: why shouldst thou seeke to slay him?
He lent thee wealth: to feed thy avarice?
He cal'd thee friend: what, that thou shouldst betray him?
He kist thee, though he knew his life the price:
He washt thy feet: should'st thou his sacrifice?
He gave thee bread, and wine, his bodie, blood,
And at thy heart to enter in he stood,
But then I entred in, and all my snakie brood.

As when wild Pentheus, growne madde with fear,
Whole troups of hellish haggs about him spies,
Two bloodie Sunnes stalking the duskie sphear,
And twofold Thebes runs rowling in his eyes:
Or through the scene staring Orestes flies,
With eyes flung back upon his Mothers ghost,
That, with infernall serpents all embost,
And torches quencht in blood, doth her stern sonne accost.

Such horrid gorgons, and misformed formes
Of damned fiends, flew dauncing in his heart,
That now, unable to endure their stormes,
Flie, flie, he cries, thy selfe, what ere thou art,
Hell, hell alreadie burnes in every part.
So downe into his Torturers armes he fell,
That readie stood his funeralls to yell,
And in a clowd of night to waft him quick to hell.

Yet oft he snacht, and started as he hung:
So when the senses halfe enslumb'red lie,
The headlong bodie, readie to be flung,
By the deluding phansie, from some high,
And craggie rock, recovers greedily,
And clasps the yeelding pillow, halfe asleepe,
And, as from heav'n it tombled to the deepe,
Feeles a cold sweat through every trembling member creepe.

Thear let him hang, embowelled in blood,
Whear never any gentle Sheapheard feed
His blessed flocks, nor ever heav'nly flood
Fall on the cursed ground, nor holesome seed
That may the least delight or pleasure breed:
Let never Spring visit his habitation,
But nettles, kixe, and all the weedie nation,
With emptie elders grow, sad signes of desolation.

Thear let the Dragon keepe his habitance,
And stinking karcases be throwne avaunt,
Faunes, Sylvans, and deformed Satyrs daunce,
Wild-cats, wolves, toads, and s[c]reechowles direly chaunt,
Thear ever let some restles spirit haunt,
With hollow sound, and clashing cheynes, to scarr
That passenger, and eyes like to the starr,
That sparkles in the crest of angrie Mars afarr.

But let the blessed deawes for ever showr
Upon that ground, in whose faire fields I spie
The bloodie ensigne of our Saviour:

Strange conquest, whear the Conquerour must die,
And he is slaine, that winns the victorie:
But he, that living, had no house to owe it,
Now had no grave, but Joseph must bestowe it,
O runne ye Saints apace, and with sweete flo[w'r]s bestrowe it.

And ye glad Spirits, that now sainted sit
On your coelestiall thrones, in beawtie drest,
Though I your teares recoumpt, O let not it
With after-sorrowe wound your tender brest,
Or with new griefe unquiet your soft rest:
Inough is me your plaints to sound againe,
That never could inough my selfe complaine,
Sing then, O sing aloude thou Arimathean Swaine.

But long he stood, in his faint armes uphoulding
The fairest spoile heav'n ever forfeited,
With such a silent passion griefe unfoulding,
That, had the sheete but on himselfe beene spread,
He for the corse might have beene buried:
And with him stood the happie theefe, that stole
By night his owne salvation, and a shole
Of Maries drowned, round about him, sat in dole.

At length (kissing his lipps before he spake,
At if from thence he fetcht againe his ghost)
To Mary thus, with teares, his silence brake.
Ah woefull soule! what joy in all our cost,
When him we hould, we have alreadie lost?
Once did'st thou loose thy Sonne, but found'st againe,
Now find'st thy Sonne, but find'st him lost, and slaine.
Ay mee! though he could death, how canst thou life sustaine?

Whear ere, deere Lord, thy Shadowe hovereth,
Blessing the place, wherein it deigns abide,
Looke how the earth darke horrour covereth,
Cloathing in mournfull black her naked side,
Willing her shadowe up to heav'n to glide,
To see and if it meet thee wandring thear,
That so, and if her selfe must misse thee hear,
At least her shadow may her dutie to thee bear.

See how the Sunne in daytime cloudes his face,
And lagging Vesper, loosing his late teame,
Forgets in heav'n to runne his nightly race,
But, sleeping on bright Oetas top, doeth dreame
The world a Chaos is, no joyfull beame
Looks from his starrie bowre, the heav'ns doe mone,

And Trees drop teares, least we should greeve alone,
The windes have learnt to sigh, and waters hoarcely grone.

And you sweete flow'rs, that in this garden growe,
Whose happie states a thousand soules envie,
Did you your owne felicities but knowe,
Your selves unpluckt would to his funerals hie,
You never could in better season die:
O that I might into your places slide,
The gate of heav'n stands gaping in his side,
Thear in my soule should steale, and all her faults should hide.

Are theas the eyes, that made all others blind;
Ah why ar they themselves now blemished?
Is this the face, in which all beawtie shin'd;
What blast hath thus his flowers debellished?
Ar these the feete, that on the watry head
Of the unfaithfull Ocean passage found;
Why goe they now so lowely under ground,
Wash't with our woorthles teares, and their owne precious wound?

One hem but of the garments that he wore,
Could medicine whole countries of their paine,
One touch of this pale hand could life restore,
One word of these cold lips revive the slaine:
Well the blinde man thy Godhead might maintaine,
What though the sullen Pharises repin'd?
He that should both compare, at length would finde
The blinde man onely sawe, the Seers all wear blinde.

Why should they thinke thee worthy to be slaine?
Was it because thou gav'st their blinde men eyes;
Or that thou mad'st their lame to walke againe;
Or for thou heal'dst their sick mens maladies;
Or mad'st their dumbe to speake; and dead to rise?
O could all these but any grace have woon,
What would they not to save thy life have done?
The dumb man would have spoke, and lame man would have runne.

Let mee, O let me neere some fountaine lie,
That through the rocke heaves up his sandie head,
Or let me dwell upon some mountaine high,
Whose hollowe root, and baser parts ar spread
On fleeting waters, in his bowells bred,
That I their streames, and they my teares may feed,
Or, cloathed in some Hermits ragged weed,
Spend all my daies, in weeping for this cursed deed.

The life, the which I once did love, I leave,
The love, in whi[c]h I once did live, I loath,
I hate the light, that did my light bereave,
Both love, and life, I doe despise you both,
O that one grave might both our ashes cloath!
A Love, a Life, a Light I now obteine,
Able to make my Age growe young againe,
Able to save the sick, and to revive the slaine.

Thus spend we teares, that never can be spent,
On him, that sorrow now no more shall see:
Thus send we sighs, that never can be sent,
To him, that died to live, and would not be,
To be thear whear he would; here burie we
This heav'nly earth, here let it softly sleepe,
The fairest Sheapheard of the fairest sheepe.
So all the bodie kist, and homewards went to weepe.

So home their bodies went, to seeke repose,
But at the grave they left their soules behinde;
O who the force of love coelestiall knowes!
That can the cheynes of natures selfe unbinde,
Sending the Bodie home, without the minde.
Ah blessed Virgin, what high Angels art
Can ever coumpt thy teares, or sing thy smart,
When every naile, that pierst his hand, did pierce thy heart?

So Philomel, perch't on an aspin sprig,
Weeps all the night her lost virginitie,
And sings her sad tale to the merrie twig,
That daunces at such joyfull miserie,
Ne ever lets sweet rest invade her eye:
But leaning on a thorne her daintie chest,
For feare soft sleepe should steale into her brest,
Expresses in her song greefe not to be exprest.

So when the Larke, poore birde, afarre espi'th
Her yet unfeather'd children (whom to save
She strives in vaine) slaine by the fatall sithe,
Which from the medowe her greene locks doeth shave,
That their warme nest is now become their grave;
The woefull mother up to heaven springs,
And all about her plaintive notes she flings,
And their untimely fate most pittifully sings.

CANTO IV

Thear all alone she spi'd, alas the while;
In shadie darknes a poore Desolate,
That now had measur'd many a wearie mile,
Through a wast desert, whither heav'nly fate,
And his owne will him brought; he praying sate,
And him to prey, as he to pray began,
The Citizens of the wilde forrest ran,
And all with open throat would swallowe whole the man.

Soone did the Ladie to her Graces crie,
And on their wings her selfe did nimbly strowe,
After her coach a thousand Loves did flie,
So downe into the wildernesse they throwe,
Whear she, and all her trayne that with her flowe
Thorough the ayrie wave, with sayles so gay,
Sinking into his brest that wearie lay,
Made shipwracke of themselves, and vanish't quite away.

Seemed that Man had them devoured all,
Whome to devoure the beasts did make pretence,
But him their salvage thirst did nought appall,
Though weapons none he had for his defence:
What armes for Innocence, but Innocence?
For when they saw their Lords bright cognizance
Shine in his face, soone did they disadvaunce,
And some unto him kneele, and some about him daunce.

Downe fell the Lordly Lions angrie mood,
And he himselfe fell downe, in congies lowe;
Bidding him welcome to his wastfull wood,
Sometime he kist the grasse whear he did goe,
And, as to wash his feete he well did knowe,
With fauning tongue he lickt away the dust,
And every one would neerest to him thrust,
And every one, with new, forgot his former lust.

Unmindfull of himselfe, to minde his Lord,
The Lamb stood gazing by the Tygers side,
As though betweene them they had made accord,
And on the Lions back the goate did ride,
Forgetfull of the roughnes of the hide,
If he stood still, their eyes upon him bayted,
If walk't, they all in order on him wayted,
And when he slep't, they as his watch themselves conceited.

Wonder doeth call me up to see, O no,
I cannot see, and therefore sinke in woonder,
The man, that shines as bright as God, not so,

For God he is himselfe, that close lies under
That man, so close, that no time can dissunder
That band, yet not so close, but from him breake
Such beames, as mortall eyes are all too weake
Such sight to see, or it, if they should see, to speake.

Upon a grassie hillock he was laid,
With woodie primroses befreckeled,
Over his head the wanton shadowes plaid
Of a wilde olive, that her bowgh's so spread,
As with her leav's she seem'd to crowne his head,
And her greene armes [t'] embrace the Prince of peace,
The Sunne so neere, needs must the winter cease,
The Sunne so neere, another Spring seem'd to increase.

His haire was blacke, and in small curls did twine,
As though it wear the shadowe of some light,
And underneath his face, as day, did shine,
But sure the day shined not halfe so bright,
Nor the Sunnes shadowe made so darke a night.
Under his lovely locks, her head to shroude,
Did make Humilitie her selfe growe proude,
Hither, to light their lamps, did all the Graces croude.

One of ten thousand soules I am, and more,
That of his eyes, and their sweete wounds complaine,
Sweete are the wounds of love, never so sore,
Ah might he often slaie mee so againe.
He never lives, that thus is never slaine.
What boots it watch? those eyes, for all my art,
Mine owne eyes looking on, have stole my heart,
In them Love bends his bowe, and dips his burning dart.

As when the Sunne, caught in an adverse clowde,
Flies crosse the world, and thear a new begets,
The watry picture of his beautie proude,
Throwes all abroad his sparkling spangelets,
And the whole world in dire amazement sets,
To see two dayes abroad at once, and all
Doubt whither nowe he rise, or nowe will fall:
So flam'd the Godly flesh, proude of his heav'nly thrall.

His cheekes as snowie apples, sop't in wine,
Had their red roses quencht with lillies white,
And like to garden strawberries did shine,
Wash't in a bowle of milke, or rose-buds bright
Unbosoming their brests against the light:
Here love-sicke soules did eat, thear dranke, and made

Sweete-smelling posies, that could never fade,
But worldly eyes him thought more like some living shade.

For laughter never look't upon his browe,
Though in his face all smiling joyes did bide,
No silken banners did about him flowe,
Fooles make their fetters ensignes of their pride:
He was best cloath'd when naked was his side,
A Lambe he was, and wollen fleece he bore,
Wove with one thread, his feete lowe sandalls wore,
But bared were his legges, so went the times of yore.

As two white marble pillars that uphold
Gods holy place whear he in glorie sets,
And rise with goodly grace and courage bold,
To beare his Temple on their ample jetts,
Vein'd every whear with azure rivulets,
Whom all the people on some holy morne,
With boughs and flowrie garlands doe adorne,
Of such, though fairer farre, this Temple was upborne.

Twice had Diana bent her golden bowe,
And shot from heav'n her silver shafts, to rouse
The sluggish salvages, that den belowe,
And all the day in lazie covert drouze,
Since him the silent wildernesse did house,
The heav'n his roofe, and arbour harbour was,
The ground his bed, and his moist pillowe grasse.
But fruit thear none did growe, nor rivers none did passe.

At length an aged Syre farre off he sawe
Come slowely footing, everie step he guest
One of his feete he from the grave did drawe,
Three legges he had, the woodden was the best,
And all the waie he went, he ever blest
With benedicities, and prayers store,
But the bad ground was blessed ne'r the more,
And all his head with snowe of Age was waxen hore.

A good old Hermit he might seeme to be,
That for devotion had the world forsaken,
And now was travailing some Saint to see,
Since to his beads he had himselfe betaken,
Whear all his former sinnes he might awaken,
And them might wash away with dropping brine,
And almes, and fasts, and churches discipline,
And dead, might rest his bones under the holy shrine.

But when he neerer came, he lowted lowe
With prone obeysance, and with curt'sie kinde,
That at his feete his head he seemd to throwe;
What needs him now another Saint to finde?
Affections are the sailes, and faith the wind,
That to this Saint a thousand soules conveigh
Each hour': O happy Pilgrims thither strey!
What caren they for beasts, or for the wearie way?

Soone the old Palmer his devotions sung,
Like pleasing anthems, moduled in time,
For well that aged Syre could tip his tongue
With golden foyle of eloquence, and lime,
And licke his rugged speech with phrases prime.
Ay me, quoth he, how many yeares have beene,
Since these old eyes the Sunne of heav'n have seene!
Certes the Sonne of heav'n they now behold I weene.

Ah, mote my humble cell so blessed be
As heav'n to welcome in his lowely roofe,
And be the Temple for thy deitie!
Loe how my cottage worships thee aloofe,
That under ground hath hid his head, in proofe
It doth adore thee with the feeling lowe,
Here honie, milke, and chesnuts wild doe growe,
The boughs a bed of leaves upon thee shall bestowe.

But oh, he said, and therewith sigh't full deepe,
The heav'ns, alas, too envious are growne,
Because our fields thy presence from them keepe;
For stones doe growe, where corne was lately sowne:
(So stooping downe, he gather'd up a stone)
But thou with corne canst make this stone to eare.
What needen we the angrie heav'ns to feare?
Let them envie us still, so we enjoy thee here.

Thus on they wandred, but those holy weeds
A monstrous Serpent, and no man did cover.
So under greenest hearbs the Adder feeds:
And round about that stinking corps did hover
The dismall Prince of gloomie night, and over
His ever-damned head the Shadowes err'd
Of thousand peccant ghosts, unseene, unheard,
And all the Tyrant feares, and all the Tyrant fear'd.

He was the Sonne of blackest Acheron,
Whear many frozen soules doe chattring lie,
And rul'd the burning waves of Phlegethon,

Whear many more in flaming sulphur frie,
At once compel'd to live and forc't to die,
Whear nothing can be heard for the loud crie
Of oh, and ah, and out alas that I
Or once againe might live, or once at length might die.

Ere long they came neere to a balefull bowre,
Much like the mouth of that infernall cave,
That gaping stood all Commers to devoure,
Darke, dolefull, dreary, like a greedy grave,
That still for carrion carkasses doth crave.
The ground no hearbs, but venomous did beare,
Nor ragged trees did leave, but every whear
Dead bones, and skulls wear cast, and bodies hanged wear.

Upon the roofe the bird of sorrowe sat
Elonging joyfull day with her sad note,
And through the shady aire, the fluttring bat
Did wave her leather sayles, and blindely flote,
While with her wings the fatall S[c]reechowle smote
Th' unblessed house, thear, on a craggy stone,
Celeno hung, and made his direfull mone,
And all about the murdered ghosts did shreek, and grone.

Like clowdie moonshine, in some shadowie grove,
Such was the light in which Despaire did dwell,
But he himselfe with night for darkenesse strove.
His blacke uncombed locks dishevell'd fell
About his face, through which, as brands of hell,
Sunk in his skull, his staring eyes did glowe,
That made him deadly looke, their glimpse did showe
Like Cockatrices eyes, that sparks of poyson throwe.

His cloaths wear ragged clouts, with thornes pind fast,
And as he musing lay, to stonie fright
A thousand wilde Chimera's would him cast:
As when a fearefull dreame, in mid'st of night,
Skips to the braine, and phansies to the sight
Some winged furie, strait the hasty foot,
Eger to flie, cannot plucke up his root,
The voyce dies in the tongue, and mouth gapes without boot.

Now he would dreame that he from heaven fell,
And then would snatch the ayre, afraid to fall;
And now he thought he sinking was to hell,
And then would grasp the earth, and now his stall
Him seemed hell, and then he out would crawle,
And ever, as he crept, would squint aside,

Lest him, perhaps, some Furie had espide,
And then, alas, he should in chaines for ever bide.

Therefore he softly shrunke, and stole away,
Ne ever durst to drawe his breath for feare,
Till to the doore he came, and thear he lay
Panting for breath, as though his dying were,
And still he thought, he felt their craples teare
Him by the heels backe to his ougly denne,
Out faine he would have leapt abroad, but then
The heav'n, as hell, he fear'd, that punish guilty men.

Within the gloomie hole of this pale wight
The Serpent woo'd him with his charmes to inne,
Thear he might baite the day, and rest the night,
But under that same baite a fearefull grin
Was readie to intangle him in sinne.
But he upon ambrosia daily fed,
That grew in Eden, thus he answered,
So both away wear caught, and to the Temple fled.

Well knewe our Saviour this the Serpent was,
And the old Serpent knewe our Saviour well,
Never did any this in falshood passe,
Never did any him in truth excell:
With him we fly to heav'n, from heav'n we fell
With him: but nowe they both together met
Upon the sacred pinnacles, that threat
With their aspiring tops, Astraeas starrie seat.

Here did Presumption her pavillion spread,
Over the Temple, the bright starres among,
(Ah that her foot should trample on the head
Of that most reverend place!) and a lewd throng
Of wanton boyes sung her a pleasant song
Of love, long life, of mercie, and of grace,
And every one her deerely did embrace,
And she herselfe enamour'd was of her owne face.

A painted face, belied with vermeyl store,
Which light Euelpis every day did trimme,
That in one hand a guilded anchor wore,
Not fixed on the rocke, but on the brimme
Of the wide aire she let it loosely swimme:
Her other hand a sprinkle carried,
And ever, when her Ladie wavered,
Court-holy water all upon her sprinkeled.

Poore foole, she thought herselfe in wondrous price
With God, as if in Paradise she wear,
But, wear shee not in a fooles paradise,
She might have seene more reason to despere:
But him she, like some ghastly fiend, did feare,
And therefore as that wretch hew'd out his cell
Under the bowels, in the heart of hell,
So she above the Moone, amid the starres would dwell.

Her Tent with sunny cloudes was seel'd aloft,
And so exceeding shone with a false light,
That heav'n it selfe to her it seemed oft,
Heav'n without cloudes to her deluded sight,
But cloudes withouten heav'n it was aright,
And as her house was built, so did her braine
Build castles in the aire, with idle paine,
But heart she never had in all her body vaine.

Like as a ship, in which no ballance lies,
Without a Pilot, on the sleeping waves,
Fairely along with winde, and water flies,
And painted masts with silken sayles embraves,
That Neptune selfe the bragging vessell saves,
To laugh a while at her so proud aray;
Her waving streamers loosely shee lets play,
And flagging colours shine as bright as smiling day;

But all so soone as heav'n his browes doth bend,
Shee veils her banners, and pulls in her beames,
The emptie barke the raging billows send
Up to th' Olympique waves, and Argus seemes
Againe to ride upon our lower streames:
Right so Presumption did her selfe behave,
Tossed about with every stormie wave,
And in white lawne shee went, most like an Angel brave.

Gently our Saviour shee began to shrive,
Whither he wear the Sonne of God, or no;
For any other shee disdeign'd to wive:
And if he wear, shee bid him fearles throw
Himselfe to ground, and thearwithall did show
A flight of little Angels, that did wait
Upon their glittering wings, to latch him strait,
And longed on their backs to feele his glorious weight.

But when she saw her speech prevailed nought,
Her selfe she tombled headlong to the flore:
But him the Angels on their feathers caught,

And to an ayrie mountaine nimbly bore,
Whose snowie shoulders, like some chaulkie shore,
Restles Olympus seem'd to rest upon
With all his swimming globes: so both are gone,
The Dragon with the Lamb. Ah, unmeet Paragon.

All suddenly the hill his snowe devours,
In liew whereof a goodly garden grew,
As if the snow had melted into flow'rs,
Which their sweet breath in subtill vapours threw,
That all about perfumed spirits flew.
For what so ever might aggrate the sense,
In all the world, or please the appetence,
Heer it was powred out in lavish affluence.

Not lovely Ida might with this compare,
Though many streames his banks besilvered,
Though Xanthus with his golden sands he bare,
Nor Hibla, though his thyme depastured,
As fast againe with honie blossomed.
Ne Rhodope, ne Tempes flowrie playne,
Adonis garden was to this but vayne,
Though Plato on his beds a flood of praise did rayne.

For in all these, some one thing most did grow,
But in this one, grew all things els beside,
For sweet varietie herselfe did throw
To every banke, here all the ground she dide
In lillie white, there pinks eblazed wide;
And damask't all the earth, and here shee shed
Blew violets, and there came roses red,
And every sight the yeelding sense, as captive led.

The garden like a Ladie faire was cut,
That lay as if shee slumber'd in delight,
And to the open skies her eyes did shut;
The azure fields of heav'n wear sembled right
In a large round, set with the flo[w'r]s of light,
The flo[w'r]s-de-luce, and the round sparks of deaw,
That hung upon their azure leaves, did shew
Like twinkling starrs, that sparkle in th[e] eav'ning blew.

Upon a hillie banke her head shee cast,
On which the bowre of Vaine-Delight was built,
White, and red roses for her face wear plac't,
And for her tresses Marigolds wear spilt:
Them broadly shee displaid, like flaming guilt,
Till in the ocean the glad day wear drown'd,

Then up againe her yellow locks she wound,
And with greene fillets in their prettie calls them bound.

What should I here depeint her lillie hand,
Her veines of violets, her ermine brest,
Which thear in orient colours living stand,
Or how her gowne with silken leaves is drest;
Or how her watchmen, arm'd with boughie crest,
A wall of prim hid in his bushes bears,
Shaking at every winde their leavie spears,
While she supinely sleeps, ne to be waked fears?

Over the hedge depends the graping Elme,
Whose greener head, empurpuled in wine,
Seemed to wonder at his bloodie helme,
And halfe suspect the bunches of the vine,
Least they, perhaps, his wit should undermine.
For well he knewe such fruit he never bore:
But her weake armes embraced him the more,
And with her ruby grapes laught at her paramour.

Under the shadowe of these drunken elmes
A Fountaine rose, where Pangloretta uses,
(When her some flood of fancie overwhelms,
And one of all her favourites she chuses)
To bath herselfe, whom she in lust abuses,
And from his wanton body sucks his soule,
Which drown'd in pleasure, in that shaly bowle,
And swimming in delight, doth am[o]rously rowle.

The font of silver was, and so his showrs
In silver fell, onely the guilded bowles
(Like to a fornace, that the min'rall powres)
Seem'd to have moul't it in their shining holes:
And on the water, like to burning coles,
On liquid silver, leaves of roses lay:
But when Panglorie here did list to play,
Rose water then it ranne, and milke it rain'd they say.

The roofe thicke cloudes did paint, from which three boyes
Three gaping mermaides with their eawrs did feede,
Whose brests let fall the streame, with sleepie noise,
To Lions mouths, from whence it leapt with speede,
And in the rosie laver seem'd to bleed.
The naked boyes unto the waters fall,
Their stonie nightingales had taught to call,
When Zephyr breath'd into their watry interall.

And all about, embayed in soft sleepe,
A heard of charmed beasts aground wear spread,
Which the faire Witch in goulden chaines did keepe,
And them in willing bondage fettered,
Once men they liv'd, but now the men were dead,
And turn'd to beasts, so fabled Homer old,
That Circe, with her potion, charm'd in gold,
Us'd manly soules in beastly bodies to immould.

Through this false Eden, to his Lemans bowre,
(Whome thousand soules devoutly idolize)
Our first destroyer led our Saviour.
Thear in the lower roome, in solemne wise,
They daunc't a round, and powr'd their sacrifice
To plumpe Lyaeus, and among the rest,
The jolly Priest, in yvie garlands drest,
Chaunted wild Orgialls, in honour of the feast.

Others within their arbours swilling sat,
(For all the roome about was arboured)
With laughing Bacchus, that was growne so fat,
That stand he could not, but was carried,
And every evening freshly watered,
To quench his fierie cheeks, and all about
Small cocks broke through the wall, and sallied out
Flaggons of wine, to set on fire that spueing rout.

This their inhumed soules esteem'd their wealths,
To crowne the bouzing kan from day to night,
And sicke to drinke themselves with drinking healths,
Some vomiting, all drunken with delight.
Hence to a loft, carv'd all in yvorie white,
They came, whear whiter Ladies naked went,
Melted in pleasure, and soft languishment,
And sunke in beds of roses, amourous glaunces sent.

Flie, flie thou holy child that wanton roome,
And thou my chaster Muse those harlots shun,
And with him to a higher storie come,
Whear mounts of gold, and flouds of silver run,
The while the owners, with their wealth undone,
Starve in their store, and in their plentie pine,
Tumbling themselves upon their heaps of mine.
Glutting their famish't soules with the deceitfull shine.

Ah, who was he such pretious perills found?
How strongly Nature did her treasures hide;
And threw upon them mountains of thicke ground,

To darke their orie lustre; but queint Pride
Hath taught her Sonnes to wound their mothers side,
And gage the depth, to search for flaring shells,
In whose bright bosome spumie Bacchus swells,
That neither heav'n, nor earth henceforth in safetie dwells.

O sacred hunger of the greedie eye,
Whose neede hath end, but no end covetise,
Emptie in fulnes, rich in povertie,
That having all things, nothing can suffice,
How thou befanciest the men most wise?
The poore man would be rich, the rich man great,
The great man King, the King, in Gods owne seat
Enthron'd, with mortal arme dares flames, and thunder threat.

Therefore above the rest Ambition sat:
His Court with glitterant pearle was all enwall'd,
And round about the wall in chaires of State,
And most majestique splendor, wear enstall'd
A hundred Kings, whose temples wear impal'd
In goulden diadems, set here, and thear
With diamounds, and gemmed every whear,
And of their golden virges none disceptred wear.

High over all, Panglories blazing throne,
In her bright turret, all of christall wrought,
Like Ph[oe]bus lampe in midst of heaven, shone:
Whose starry top, with pride infernall fraught,
Selfe-arching columns to uphold wear taught:
In which, her Image still reflected was
By the smooth christall, that most like her glasse,
In beauty, and in frailtie, did all others passe.

A Silver wande the sorceresse did sway,
And, for a crowne of gold, her haire she wore,
Onely a garland of rosebuds did play
About her locks, and in her hand, she bore
A hollowe globe of glasse, that long before,
She full of emptinesse had bladdered,
And all the world therein depictured,
Whose colours, like the rainebowe, ever vanished.

Such watry orbicles young boyes doe blowe
Out from their sopy shells, and much admire
The swimming world, which tenderly they rowe
With easie breath, till it be waved higher,
But if they chaunce but roughly once aspire,
The painted bubble instantly doth fall.

Here when she came, she gan for musique call,
And sung this wooing song, to welcome him withall.

Love is the blossome whear thear blowes
Every thing, that lives, or growes,
Love doth make the heav'ns to move,
And the Sun doth burne in love;
Love the strong, and weake doth yoke,
And makes the yvie climbe the oke,
Under whose shadowes Lions wilde,
Soft'ned by Love, growe tame, and mild;
Love no med'cine can appease,
He burnes the fishes in the seas,
Not all the skill his wounds can stench,
Not all the sea his fire can quench;
Love did make the bloody spear
Once a levie coat to wear,
While in his leaves thear shrouded lay
Sweete birds, for love, that sing, and play;
And of all loves joyfull flame,
I the bud, and blossome am.
Onely bend thy knee to me,
Thy wooeing, shall thy winning be.

See, see the flowers that belowe,
Now as fresh as morning blowe,
And of all, the virgin rose,
That as bright Aurora showes,
How they all unleaved die,
Loosing their virgin[i]tie:
Like unto a summer-shade,
But now borne, and now they fade.
Every thing doth passe away,
Thear is danger in delay,
Come, come gather then the rose,
Gather it, or it you lose.
All the sande of Tagus shore
Into my bosome casts his ore;
All the valleys swimming corne
To my house is yeerely borne;
Every grape, of every vine
Is gladly bruis'd to make me wine,
While ten thousand kings, as proud,
To carry up my traine, have bow'd,
And a world of Ladies send me
In my chambers to attend me:
All the starres in heav'n that shine,
And ten thousand more, are mine:

Onely bend thy knee to mee,
Thy wooing shall thy winning bee.

Thus sought the dire Enchauntress in his minde
Her guilefull bayt to have embosomed,
But he her charmes dispersed into winde,
And her of insolence admonished,
And all her optique glasses shattered.
So with her Syre to hell shee tooke her flight,
(The starting ayre flew from the damned spright,)
Whear deeply both aggriev'd, plunged themselves in night.

But to their Lord, now musing in his thought,
A heavenly volie of light Angels flew,
And from his Father him a banquet brought,
Through the fine element, for well they knew,
After his lenten fast, he hungrie grew,
And, as he fed, the holy quires combine
To sing a hymne of the celestiall Trine;
All thought to passe, and each was past all thought divine.

The birds sweet notes, to sonnet out their joyes,
Attemper'd to the layes Angelicall,
And to the birds, the winds attune their noyse,
And to the winds, the waters hoarcely call,
And Eccho back againe revoyced all,
That the whole valley rung with victorie.
But now our Lord to rest doth homewards flie:
See how the Night comes stealing from the mountains high.

www.ingramcontent.com/pod-product-compliance
Lightning Source LLC
Chambersburg PA
CBHW060056050426
42448CB00011B/2482